By Paul Shipton
Illustrated by Matteo Piana
Activities by Hannah Fish

Contents

Meet the Characters
Hello! My name is Rosie. This is my brother.
Hi! I'm Ben. This is Grandpa.
And here's Grandpa's fantastic van.
It can go anywhere!

Grandpa
Ben and Rosie's grandfather
Ben
Rosie's brother
Rosie
Ben's sister
Clunk
Grandpa's robot
Max and Alice
Ben and Rosie's friends
Nicole
A park ranger
Imagine!
Now let's read this story, *Bats!*

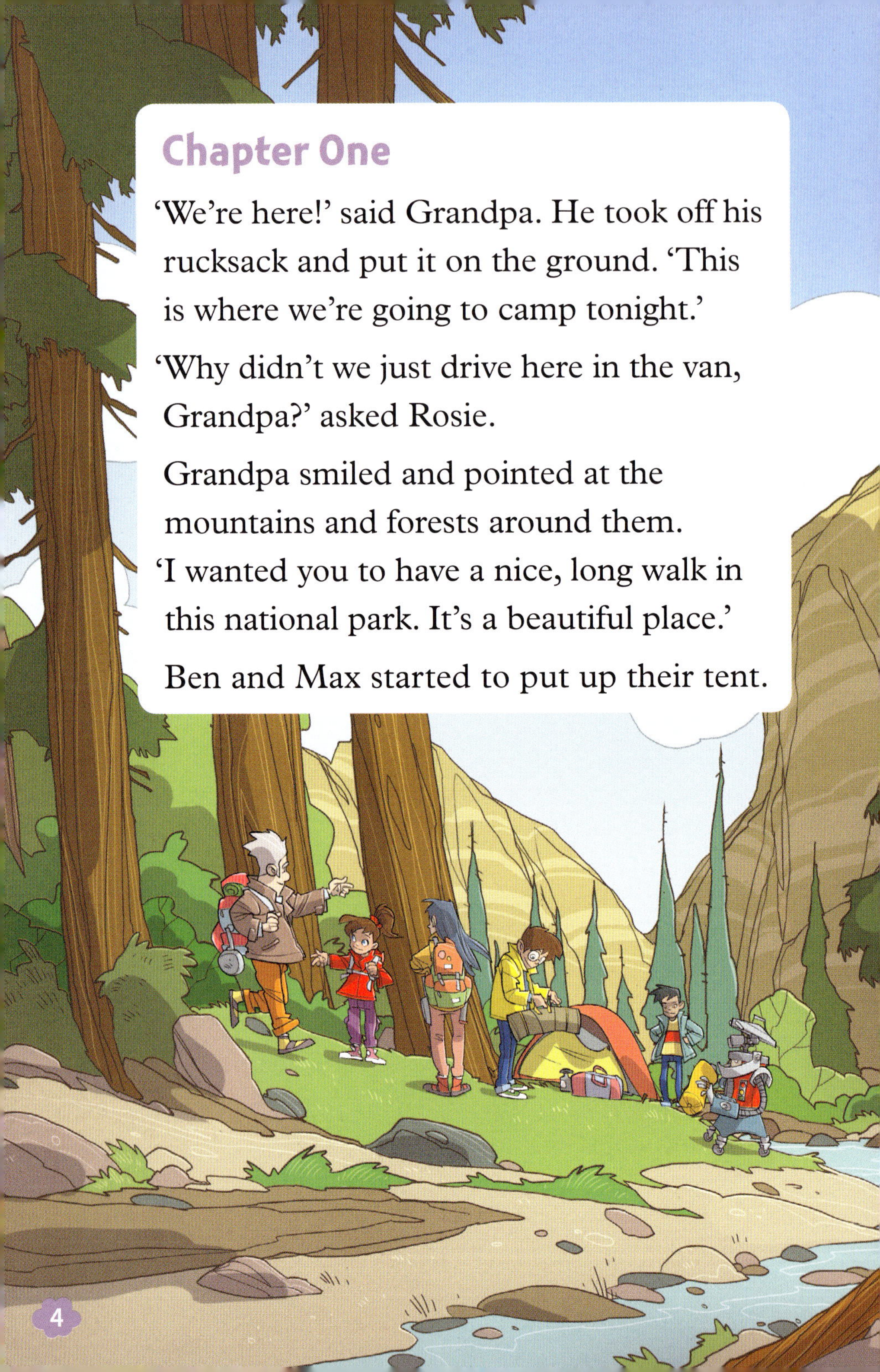

Chapter One

‘We’re here!’ said Grandpa. He took off his rucksack and put it on the ground. ‘This is where we’re going to camp tonight.’

‘Why didn’t we just drive here in the van, Grandpa?’ asked Rosie.

Grandpa smiled and pointed at the mountains and forests around them. ‘I wanted you to have a nice, long walk in this national park. It’s a beautiful place.’

Ben and Max started to put up their tent.

Soon the children heard the sound of a pickup truck. Grandpa went to meet the driver.

‘This is Nicole. She’s a park ranger,’ Grandpa told the children. ‘She knows all about the animals in this national park. She’s going to tell us about one very interesting animal.’

‘Which animal?’ asked Ben.

‘Bats,’ said Nicole with a big smile.

→ Go to page 24 for activities.

'I hate bats!' said Rosie. 'They're frightening.'

'No, they're not!' said Ben.

'Bats are amazing,' said Nicole. 'They fly at night and they use sound to catch their food.'

'How?' asked Alice.

'They make a sound as they fly,' explained Nicole. 'When the sound hits a bug, it bounces back to the bat. Then the bat knows where the bug is!'

‘Wait a minute,’ said Rosie. ‘Bugs? Are there bugs here that will bite us?’

‘There are lots of mosquitoes around here at night,’ said Grandpa, ‘but don’t worry – we’ve got mosquito spray.’

‘Oh dear!’ said Clunk. ‘I forgot the mosquito spray. It’s still in the van.’

‘But the van’s far away!’ said Max.

‘That’s OK,’ said Clunk. ‘I’ll go and get the spray.’

The little robot started to go back to the van.

Go to page 26 for activities.

Chapter Two

Grandpa was looking in his rucksack.

'The marshmallows are in the van, too,' he said. 'Ben and Rosie, can you go tell Clunk, please?'

'Yes,' said Rosie. 'We'll go to the van with him.'

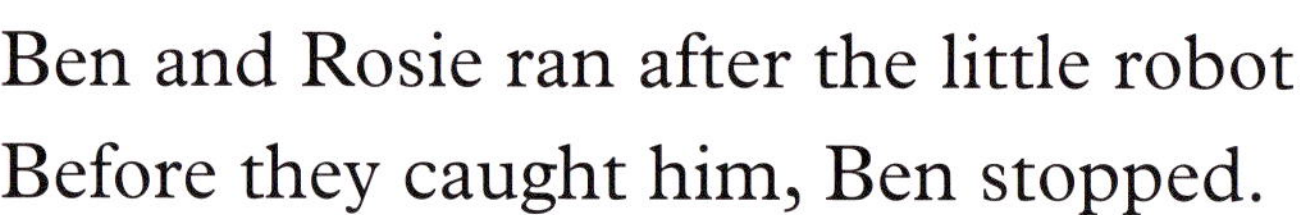

Ben and Rosie ran after the little robot. Before they caught him, Ben stopped.

'Rosie,' he said. 'Look at this!'

He was pointing at a small cave.

'Let's have a look inside,' Ben said.

'We have to catch Clunk,' said Rosie.

'We'll only be a minute,' said Ben. 'We can use my cell phone as a flashlight.' He looked at his little sister. 'Or are you frightened?'

'No!' said Rosie. 'We can have a *quick* look inside.'

The light from Ben's phone was strong, but it was still very dark in the cave.

'Please can we go find Clunk now?' said Rosie.

'Just a little more,' said Ben.

Go to page 28 for activities.

Suddenly, there was a sound. Something black was moving quickly in the dark.

'A bat!' shouted Rosie. She jumped when the bat flew close to her.

'It's OK –' Ben started to say, but he couldn't say any more. There was a hole in the floor of the dark cave that the children didn't know about. As Rosie jumped, she and Ben fell into the hole.

A second later, they hit hard rock.

'Are you OK?' Ben asked.

'Yes,' answered Rosie. 'But how are we going to get out of here?'

Ben stood up and looked around by the light of his phone.

They were in another cave now, and this one went down into the mountain. 'We can't climb back up,' Ben said. 'I hurt my arm when I fell.'

→ Go to page 30 for activities.

Chapter Three

The children shouted and shouted for help.

'Nobody can hear us,' said Rosie at last.

'And I can't use my cell phone here,' said Ben. 'Grandpa thinks that we're with Clunk. He won't look for us until Clunk comes back.' He looked around. 'There are lots of caves in this mountain. We just have to find a different way out. Come on, Rosie.'

The children walked and walked in the dark. Sometimes they went up, and sometimes down. Sometimes they went left, and sometimes right.

'Is this the right way?' asked Rosie.

'I think it is,' said Ben.

At last, they came to a much bigger cave.

'There isn't a way out!' said Ben.

'Wait,' said Rosie. She put a hand on her brother's arm. 'I can hear something!'

→ Go to page 32 for activities.

Carefully, Ben moved the light from his phone so they could see better.

'Look!' said Rosie quietly.
'There are bats – hundreds of them!'

'Maybe *thousands*,' said Ben.

The bats were hanging upside down and sleeping everywhere.

Slowly, Ben began to move back.
'Let's go,' he said. 'We don't want to be here when they wake up.'

'You're wrong,' said Rosie.
'We *do* want to be here then. I have an idea ...'

Outside, the sun was going down.

Max looked at his watch. 'Where *are* they?' he asked. 'I wanted to make the fire with Ben.'

Suddenly, there was a happy shout: 'I'm back! I've brought the mosquito spray, and I have the marshmallows, too!' It was Clunk.

'Great,' said Alice. 'But where are Rosie and Ben?'

Clunk stopped. 'I don't understand,' he said. 'Rosie and Ben didn't come with me.'

Go to page 34 for activities.

Chapter Four

Max and Alice were afraid – where were their friends?

'Clunk didn't see or hear them in the forest,' said Nicole. 'Perhaps they're in one of the caves.'

'But there are many kilometers of caves here,' said Grandpa.

'I know.' Nicole was already running to her pickup truck. 'I have flashlights and ropes,' she said. 'Come on. We can't wait – it's going to be dark soon!'

Suddenly, Max shouted, 'Look at that!'

He was pointing to a place up the mountain. Alice turned and saw hundreds of small, black shapes. They were flying fast, out into the evening sky.

'It's the bats!' said Nicole. 'They've woken up to look for their food.'

Grandpa didn't look up. He was frightened and wanted to find Ben and Rosie. But where should they begin to look?

→ Go to page 36 for activities.

Ben and Rosie waited outside the bats' cave. They listened carefully.

'Have all the bats gone?' Rosie asked.

'I think they have,' said Ben.

Rosie smiled in the dark. 'That means that there's a hole to the outside world. If we find it, we can leave.'

'Great idea, Rosie!' said Ben. 'But will the hole be big enough?'

'We have another problem,' Ben said.

He looked down at the phone in his hand. Its light was getting weaker and weaker.

'How can we find the hole in this big cave without a light?' asked Rosie.

Ben took Rosie's hand. 'I know!' he said. 'Come on!'

Inside the cave, Ben shouted loudly: 'HELLO!'

'What are you doing?' asked Rosie.

'I'm doing the same thing that bats do!' said Ben.

Go to page 38 for activities.

Chapter Five

Ben shouted again: ‘HELLO!’
The sound bounced back at them from the cave walls: ‘HELLO!’

He turned and shouted again: ‘HELLO!’

Again the sound came back, ‘HELLO!’

But when Ben turned and shouted for a third time, the sound didn’t bounce back to them. ‘That’s because there’s a hole in the cave wall there,’ he explained. ‘That’s the way out!’

Outside, Grandpa and Nicole were looking at a map.

'There are a lot of caves,' Grandpa said. 'Which one should we start at?'

'We don't have to,' shouted Clunk happily. 'I can see Ben and Rosie!'

The robot pointed up the mountain.

Ben and Rosie were coming out of the same hole as the bats.

→ Go to page 40 for activities.

When they arrived at the tents, Ben said, 'I'm very sorry, Grandpa. We only wanted to have a quick look in the cave.'

'Caves can be dangerous,' Grandpa said. 'You must never do that again.' Then he smiled. 'You're probably both hungry now.'

'Very hungry!' said Rosie.

'OK,' said Grandpa. 'Let's make a fire and eat those marshmallows!'

Later, they all sat around the fire while Nicole told them more about bats. 'They're interesting, beautiful animals,' she said.

As she listened, Rosie looked up at the night sky. She could see little black shapes flying here and there – bats!

'I agree,' Rosie said with a smile. 'Bats *are* amazing!'

→ Go to page 42 for activities.

Activities for pages 4–5

1 Match.

1 camp
2 national park
3 tent
4 mountain
5 rucksack
6 forest

2 Complete the sentences.

camp meet ~~took off~~ heard put up tell

1 Grandpa took off his rucksack and put it down.
2 They were going to ____________ in the national park.
3 Ben and Max ____________ their tent.
4 They ____________ the sound of a pickup truck.
5 Grandpa went to ____________ the park ranger.
6 The park ranger was going to ____________ them about bats.

3 Circle the correct words.

1 Grandpa pointed at the mountains and **animals** / **forests**.

2 They were in a **national park** / **pickup truck**.

3 The national park was a beautiful **sound** / **place**.

4 Nicole was driving a **van** / **pickup truck**.

5 Nicole was a **van driver** / **park ranger**.

6 Nicole knew all about the **animals** / **people** in the park.

7 Nicole was going to tell them about **bats** / **rabbits**.

4 Look at the picture on page 5 and write *yes* or *no*.

1 Nicole is wearing a hat. ______

2 The tent is blue. ______

3 There are some trees. ______

4 Ben is wearing a yellow coat. ______

5 Alice is standing behind Max. ______

6 The pickup truck is green. ______

7 Rosie is talking to Nicole. ______

8 Clunk is putting up the tent. ______

Talk **Do you like bats? Talk to a friend.**

Activities for pages 6–7

1 Write the words.

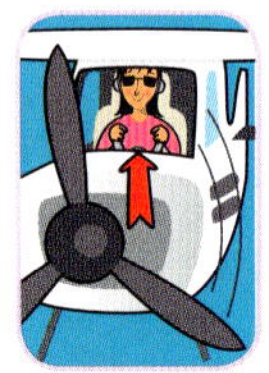

1 fly 2 ______ 3 ______

4 ______ 5 ______ 6 ______

2 Match. Then write the sentences.

1 Bats fly	as they fly.
2 Bats use sound	where the bug is.
3 They make a sound	at night.
4 The sound hits a	to catch their food.
5 Then the bat knows	bug and bounces back.

1 Bats fly at night.

2 ______

3 ______

4 ______

5 ______

3 Choose and write the correct words.

Grandpa and the children were in a [1] national park. They met a [2] ____________ called Nicole. Nicole knew all about the [3] ____________ in the park. She told the children all about bats. There were lots of [4] ____________ in the park, so Clunk went back to the van to get the mosquito [5] ____________.

park ranger	Nicole	~~national park~~	mosquitoes
bats	pickup truck	spray	animals

Now tick (✓) the best name for Chapter One.

Frightening bats! ☐

Beautiful bats! ☐

Amazing bats! ☐

Activities for pages 8–9

1 Choose and write the correct words.

marshmallows spray ~~a van~~ a robot a flashlight
a cave a rucksack a cell phone a bug

1 This is something you drive. It is bigger than a car. a van
2 You use this to help you see in the dark. You can carry it with you. ____________
3 Clunk is one of these. ____________
4 You eat these things. They are soft and sweet. ____________
5 You use this to talk to people who are not with you. ____________
6 This is a type of bag that you carry on your back. ____________
7 This is a big hole in the side of a mountain. ____________

2 Circle the correct answer.

Why does Ben think Rosie is frightened?

she is little the cave is dark
she wants to catch Clunk

3 Look at page 8 and complete the sentences. You can use 1, 2, 3, or 4 words.

1 Grandpa was looking for the marshmallows.

2 The marshmallows were ________ van.

3 Grandpa asked ________ to go and tell Clunk.

4 Ben and Rosie ________ after Clunk.

5 Then ________ at a small cave.

6 Ben ________ a look inside the cave.

4 Write *yes* or *no*.

1 The marshmallows were in the van. yes

2 Ben and Rosie ran after Clunk. ________

3 Ben saw a small cave. ________

4 Rosie wanted to go into the cave. ________

5 Ben had his cell phone with him. ________

6 The light from Ben's phone was strong. ________

7 The cave was very dark. ________

8 Ben wanted to find Clunk. ________

Talk **What is in the cave? Tell a friend your ideas.**

Activities for pages 10–11

1 Choose and write the correct words.

Ben and Rosie ran [1] after Clunk. Then Ben saw a cave, and he wanted [2] __________ inside. The cave was dark, but they used Ben's cell phone [3] __________ a flashlight. Suddenly, there was a bat moving in the dark. Rosie jumped, and the children fell [4] __________ a hole. They were in [5] __________ cave, and they didn't know how to get out!

1 away for ~~after~~

2 for look looking to look

3 as so at

4 up to onto into

5 another other that

2 Write the words.

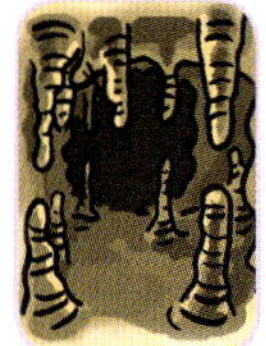

1 __________ 2 __________ 3 __________

3 Choose the best answers.

1 Rosie: I just heard something!

Ben: c

2 Rosie: Look! There is something in the dark.

Ben: ____

3 Rosie: Quick, Ben, jump!

Ben: ____

4 Rosie: Ouch! I hit something hard.

Ben: ____

5 Rosie: Yes, but how can we get out?

Ben: ____

a It's a bat!
b Did you find it?
c What was it?
d I don't know.
e It's a cave!
f Oh no! We're falling.
g Are you OK?

Talk **Can Ben and Rosie get out of the cave? Tell a friend your ideas.**

Activities for pages 12–13

1 Write the words.

1 up pu

2 ________ wond

3 ________ tefl

4 ________ ghtri

2 Order the words.

1 could / shouting. / Nobody / children / hear / the

Nobody could hear the children shouting.

2 way / had / They / to find / out. / just / a different

____

3 in / The / dark. / walked / the / children

____

4 bigger / came / Then / to a / they / cave.

____

5 Rosie / hear / But / something. / could

____

3 Circle the mistakes. Then write the correct words.

1 The children shouted of help. for

2 Ben couldn't use he's cell phone. ______

3 Grandpa wouldn't look for the children. ______

4 The children went up and down, left and write. ______

5 Then they came to a more bigger cave. ______

6 Rosie put her hand on Bens arm. ______

7 Rosie could hearing something. ______

4 Order the events.

Rosie told Ben to wait. ___

The children walked in the dark. ___

The children shouted for help. 1

At last, they came to a bigger cave. ___

Rosie could hear something. ___

Ben looked around and said, 'Come on, Rosie.' ___

Talk What can Rosie hear? Tell a friend your ideas.

Activities for pages 14–15

1 Circle the odd one out.

1 carefully / slowly / light
2 thousands / mosquito / hundreds
3 upside down / down / so
4 sleep / wake up / shout
5 fire / hang / marshmallow
6 bring / look / see
7 Alice / Clunk / Ben

2 Circle the correct answers.

1 How many bats were there?

a hundred   under a hundred   more than a hundred

2 How were the bats hanging?

in a line   on a door   upside down

3 Who had an idea?

Ben   Rosie

4 What time of day was it?

morning   evening

3 Who said this? Write the names.

1 'There are bats – hundreds of them!' Rosie

2 'Rosie and Ben didn't come with me.' ________

3 'Maybe *thousands*.' ________

4 'But where are Rosie and Ben?' ________

5 'I wanted to make the fire with Ben.' ________

6 'We don't want to be here when they wake up.' ________

7 'We *do* want to be here then.' ________

4 Read the summary of Chapter Three. Write the missing words.

The children shouted, but [1] nobody could hear them. They had to find a different way out. They walked and walked in the dark. At last, they came to a [2] ________ cave. In the cave there were hundreds of [3] ________. Maybe thousands! The bats were hanging upside down and sleeping. Rosie had an idea. Outside, Max looked at his watch. He wanted to make the fire with [4] ________. Clunk came back with the [5] ________ spray and marshmallows, but Alice said, 'Where are Rosie and Ben?'

Talk **What is Rosie's idea? Tell a friend your ideas.**

Activities for pages 16–17

1 Match.

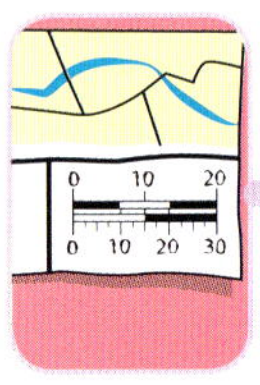

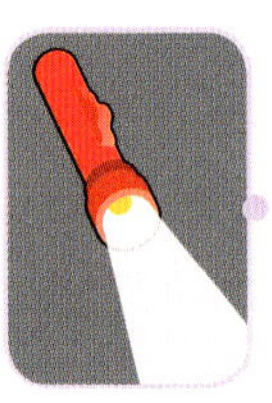

1 rope

2 kilometer

3 flashlight

2 Look at pages 16 and 17 and complete the sentences. You can use 1, 2, 3, or 4 words.

1 Max ________________ were afraid.

2 They didn't ________________ Rosie were.

3 There were many kilometers ________________ the national park.

4 Nicole had ________________ and ropes in the back of her truck.

5 It ________________ dark soon.

6 Suddenly, Max pointed to a place ________________ mountain.

7 Small, black shapes were ________________ fast.

8 It was the bats. They had ________________ to look for food.

Talk **Can they find Ben and Rosie? Tell a friend your ideas.**

3 Choose the best answers.

1 Grandpa: Where are Ben and Rosie?

Nicole: ____

2 Rosie: What should we do?

Nicole: ____

3 Rosie: Do you have any flashlights?

Nicole: ____

4 Rosie: OK. Let's get them quickly.

Nicole: ____

5 Rosie: Look! What's that in the air?

Nicole: ____

a Yes, it's going to be dark soon.

b Perhaps they're in a cave.

c No, I don't have any.

d We need to find them!

e It's the bats looking for food.

f It's Max making a fire.

g Yes, they're in my pickup truck.

h What's that up there?

Activities for pages 18–19

1 Write *yes* or *no*.

1 Ben and Rosie waited in the bats' cave. ________

2 All the bats had gone. ________

3 That meant there was a hole to the outside world. ________

4 Rosie was holding Ben's cell phone. ________

5 The light from the phone was strong. ________

2 Choose and write the correct words.

Ben and Rosie listened to the bats flying away. Rosie [1] __________. 'That means there's a hole to the outside [2] __________,' she said. The children just had to find the hole. They had another problem. The [3] __________ from Ben's phone was weak. But Ben had an [4] __________. He shouted 'HELLO!' loudly.

light

world

smiled

cell phone

idea

3 Match. Then complete the sentences.

have listen find do leave is

listened did left was had found

1 Ben and Rosie listened carefully.
2 They waited until all the bats __________ gone.
3 There __________ a hole to the outside world.
4 They needed to find the hole to __________.
5 But how could they __________ the hole without a light?
6 Ben was doing the same thing that bats __________.

4 Circle the mistakes in the questions. Then write the correct words.

1 Have all the bats go? gone
2 Will the hole is big enough? __________
3 How are we find the hole without a light? __________
4 What do you doing? __________

Talk Why is Ben shouting? Tell a friend your ideas.

Activities for pages 20–21

1 Look at pages 20 and 21 and complete the sentences. You can use 1, 2, 3, or 4 words.

1 Ben ____________ again.

2 The sound ____________ them from the cave walls.

3 When Ben shouted ____________, the sound didn't bounce back.

4 There was a hole in ____________ there.

5 Grandpa and Nicole were ____________ a map.

6 But Clunk could ____________ Ben and Rosie.

7 Clunk pointed up ____________.

8 Ben and Rosie were ____________ the hole in the mountain.

2 What is it?

1 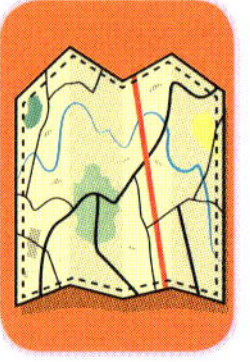 It's a ____________.

2  It's a ____________.

3 Choose and write the correct words.

Ben shouted [1] ____________. The sound bounced back [2] ____________ them from the cave walls. He shouted again [3] ____________ again. When he shouted for the [4] ____________ time, the sound didn't bounce back. They [5] ____________ found the hole in the cave wall! Outside, Grandpa and Nicole were looking [6] ____________ a map. There were a [7] ____________ of caves in the national park. But then Clunk [8] ____________ up the mountain. Ben and Rosie were [9] ____________ out of the same hole the bats flew [10] ____________!

1 about again after

2 for from to

3 but and at

4 third three again

5 have had were

6 for at to

7 lot lots a lot

8 pointing point pointed

9 came come coming

10 out of up to for

Activities for pages 22–23

1 Write the words.

w l a s m h r a o l m

1 ____________

g y n h r u

2 ____________

r f e i

3 ____________

k y s

4 ____________

2 Who said this? Write the names.

1 'I agree. Bats *are* amazing!' ____________

2 'Caves can be dangerous. You must never do that again.' ____________

3 'They're interesting, beautiful animals.' ____________

4 'I'm very sorry, Grandpa. We only wanted to have a quick look in the cave.' ____________

5 'Let's make a fire and eat those marshmallows!' ____________

3 Choose and write the correct words.

Ben shouted and the [1] __________ bounced back to them from the cave walls. But when he shouted for the third time, the sound didn't [2] __________ back. That was because there was a hole in the cave wall there. Outside, Clunk saw Ben and Rosie coming out of the hole in the [3] __________. Ben was very sorry. Now he knew that caves could be [4] __________! After dinner, [5] __________ told them more about bats, and Rosie agreed that bats are amazing!

Nicole

dangerous

rock

Rosie

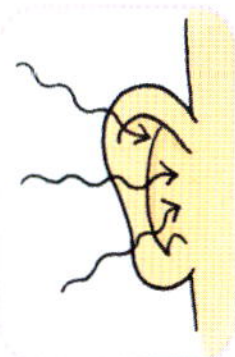
sound

mountain

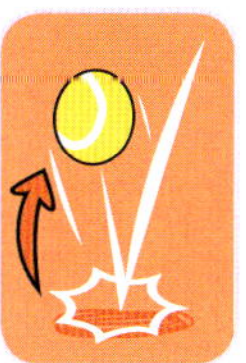
bounce

frightened

Talk **Do you like this story? Talk to a friend.**

Bat Research

What do you know about bats? Do you like them? Talk to a friend.

1 **Use the Internet to do some research on bats. Draw a picture of a bat and label it with the words in the box.**

ears wings nose teeth mouth

2 **Now use your research to answer the questions on page 45.**

What kind of animals are bats?
Are they birds?

How many kinds of bat are there?

What color are bats?

Do bats look for food in the daytime or at night?

How do bats look for food?

What do bats eat?

Do bats live in groups?

Where do bats live?

How long do bats live for?

Talk **Talk to a friend about your research. Did you find out interesting things about bats?**

Picture Dictionary

animals

bat

bounce

bugs

camp

catch

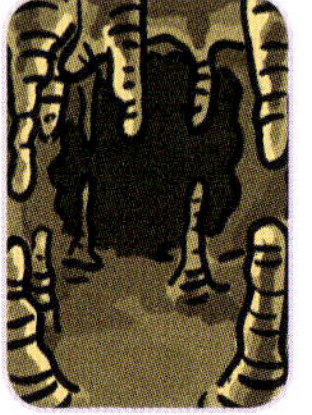

cave

cell phone

climb

fire

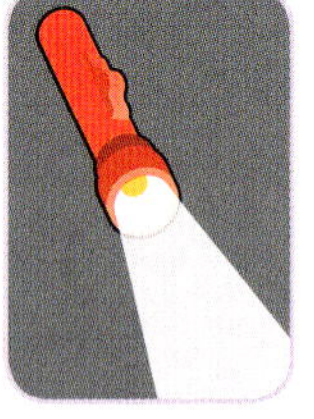

flashlight

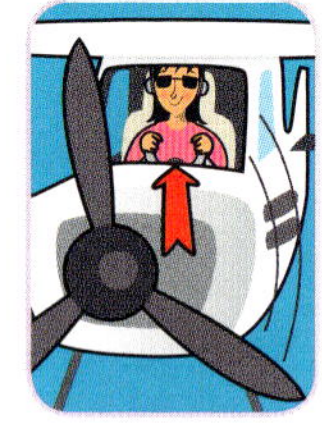

fly

forest

frightened

hang upside down

hit

hole

hungry

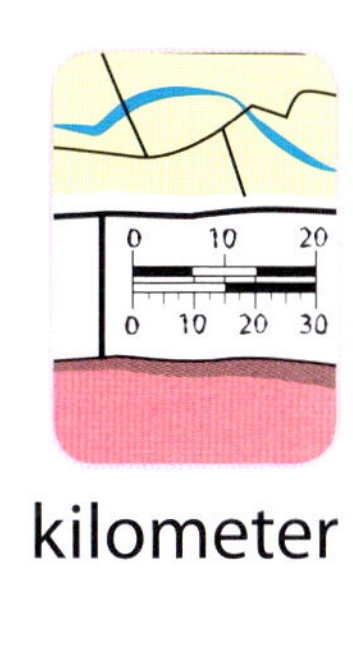

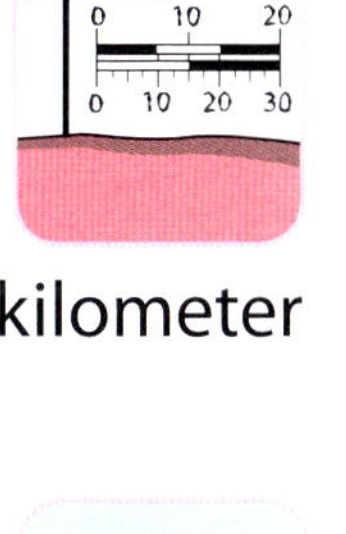

kilometer

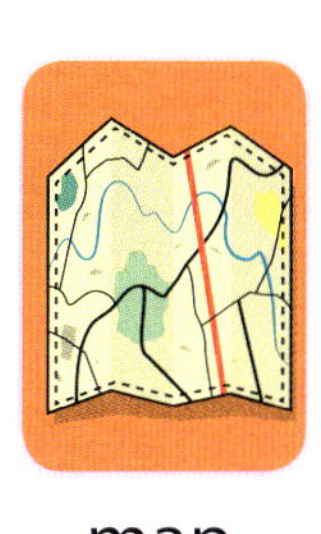

map

marshmallow

mosquito

mountain

national park

park ranger

pickup truck

rock

rope

rucksack

spray

tent

wall

Oxford Read and Imagine

Oxford Read and Imagine graded readers are at nine levels (Early Starter, Starter, Beginner, and Levels 1 to 6) for students from age 3 to 4 and older. They offer great stories to read and enjoy.

Activities provide Cambridge Young Learner Exams preparation. See Key below.

At Levels 1 to 6, every storybook reader links to an **Oxford Read and Discover** non-fiction reader, giving students a chance to find out more about the world around them, and an opportunity for Content and Language Integrated Learning (CLIL).

For more information about **Read and Imagine**, and for Teacher's Notes, go to www.oup.com/elt/teacher/readandimagine

KEY

M Activity supports Cambridge Young Learners Movers Exam preparation

F Activity supports Cambridge Young Learners Flyers Exam preparation

Oxford Read and Discover

Do you want to find out more about which animals come out at night, and what special senses nocturnal animals have? You can read this non-fiction book.

OXFORD
UNIVERSITY PRESS

Great Clarendon Street, Oxford, OX2 6DP, United Kingdom

Oxford University Press is a department of the University of Oxford. It furthers the University's objective of excellence in research, scholarship, and education by publishing worldwide. Oxford is a registered trade mark of Oxford University Press in the UK and in certain other countries

The moral rights of the author have been asserted

First published in 2016
2025 2024
12

ISBN: 978 0 19 473696 1

Printed in China

This book is printed on paper from certified and well-managed sources

ACKNOWLEDGEMENTS

Main illustrations by: Matteo Piana.

Additional illustrations by: Dusan Pavlic / Beehive illustratio[n]; Alan Rowe, Mark Ruffle.